Th Goshen Declaration

A
Declaration of Deliverance
for the
Remnant of Yisra'el

By Stephen Pidgeon

Come down unto me and tarry not; And you shall dwell in the land of Goshen, and you shall be near unto me, you, and your children, and your children's children, and your flocks, and your herds, and all that you have: And there will I nourish you; for yet there are five years of famine; lest you, and your household, and all that you have, come to poverty.

Genesis 45:9-11

ISBN-13:
978-1479179367

ISBN-10:
1479179361

And one of the scribes came, and having heard them reasoning together, and perceiving that he had answered them well, asked him, Which is the first commandment of all? And Yeshua answered him, The first of all the commandments is, Hear, O Yisra'el; YAH'HAVAH our ELOHIYM is one YAH'HAVAH: And you shall love YAH'HAVAH your ELOHIYM with all your heart, and with all your soul, and with all your mind, and with all your strength: this is the first commandment. And the second is like, namely this, You shall love your neighbour as yourself. There is none other commandment greater than these. And the scribe said unto him, Well, Master, you have said the truth: for there is one ELOHIYM; and there is none other but he: And to love him with all the heart, and with all the understanding, and with all the soul, and with all the strength, and to love his neighbour as himself, is more than all whole burnt offerings and sacrifices. And when Yeshua saw that he answered discreetly, he said unto him, You are not far from the kingdom of ELOHIYM. And no man after that dared ask him any question.

Mark 12:28-34

The Oregon Country

The land marked above was known to explorers as the Oregon Country, consisting of land north of the 42 parallel (42°N) and south of 54°40'N, west of the Rocky Mountains and to the Pacific Coast, specifically holding the mouth of the Columbia River.

We know it spiritually as *Goshen*.

Table of Contents

The banks of the river throughout are low and skirted in the distance by a chain of moderately high lands on each side, interspersed here and there with clumps of wide spreading oaks, groves of pine, and a variety of other kinds of woods. Between these high lands lie what is called the valley of the Wallamitte, the frequented haunts of innumerable herds of elk and deer.

Alexander Ross

Introduction

It is my great hope that this is going to be a short, easy to read book that will give you the information you need to see if you are called into the land of Goshen, formerly known as the Oregon Country.

This is not a place for everyone, but for those who are called out for deliverance in these last hours.

When looking out at our world and the rise of international fascism, many people are asking the question, "where can we go?" The globalists are everywhere, and yes, they have concluded that the best way to save the earth is to eliminate most of mankind.

A great tribulation is coming on the earth: famine, pestilence, war, plague, natural disasters and destruction. All of this is ordained from above, as the earth and the people on it are being judged by a righteous and holy Elohiym, who was, who is, and who is to come.

If you have been offended by the last statement, put this book down, or give it to someone you can't stand because of their weird religious beliefs.

Introduction

If you know that you are one of the called out, read on, for good news awaits.

Blessed is he whose transgression is forgiven, whose sin is covered. Blessed is the man unto whom Yah'havah does not impute iniquity, and in whose spirit there is no guile. When I kept silence, my bones waxed old through my roaring all the day long. For day and night your hand was heavy upon me: my moisture is turned into the drought of summer. Selah. I acknowledged my sin to you, and my iniquity I have not hid. I said, I will confess my transgressions unto Yah'havah; and you forgave the iniquity of my sin. Selah. For this shall every one that is Elohiymly pray to you in a time when you may be found: surely in the floods of great waters they shall not come nigh unto him.

You are my hiding place; you shall preserve me from trouble; you shall compass me about with songs of deliverance. Selah. I will instruct you and teach you in the way which you shall go: I will guide you with my eye. Be ye not as the horse, or as the mule, which have no understanding: whose mouth must be held in with bit and bridle, lest they come near unto thee. Many sorrows shall be to the wicked: but he that trusts in Yah'havah, mercy shall compass him about. Be glad in Yah'havah, and rejoice, ye righteous: and shout for joy, all ye that are upright in heart.

Psalm 32

Sing aloud unto Elohiym our strength: make a joyful noise unto the Elohiym of Jacob. Take a psalm, and bring here the timbrel, the pleasant harp with the psaltery. Blow up the shofar in the new moon, in the time appointed, on our solemn feast day. For this was a statute for Israel, and a law of the Elohiym of Jacob. This he ordained in Joseph for a testimony, when he went out through the land of Egypt: where I heard a language that I did not understand. I removed his shoulder from the burden: his hands were delivered from the pots. You called in trouble, and I delivered you; I answered you in the secret place of thunder: I proved you at the waters of Meribah. Selah.

Hear, O my people, and I will testify to you: O Israel, if you will hearken to me; There shall be no strange Elohiym in you; neither shall you worship any strange Elohiym. I am Yah'havah your Elohiym, which brought you out of the land of Egypt: open your mouth wide, and I will fill it. But my people would not hearken to my voice; and Israel would have none of me. So I gave them up unto their own hearts' lust: and they walked in their own counsels. Oh that my people had hearkened to me, and Israel had walked in my ways! I should soon have subdued their enemies, and turned my hand against their adversaries. The haters of the LORD should have submitted themselves to him: but their time should have endured forever. He should have fed them also with the finest of the wheat: and with honey out of the rock should I have satisfied them.

Psalm 81

Chapter One

The Prophecy

And it shall come to pass, that whosoever shall call on the name of YAH'HAVAH shall be delivered: for in Mount Tsyion and in Yerushalayim shall be deliverance, as YAH'HAVAH has said, and in the remnant whom YAH'HAVAH shall call.

Joel 2:32 (QCV)

Deliverance is promised for those who call on the name of Yah'havah, and Yah'havah shall call such *a remnant.*

This call to deliverance happened once before for the whole of the House of Yisra'el, when Yoseph called to his brothers:

And Yoceph said unto his brethren, Come near to me, I pray you. And they came near. And he said, I am Yoceph your brother, whom ye sold into Mitsrayim. Now therefore be not grieved, nor angry with yourselves, that ye sold me hither: for ELOHIYM did send me before you to preserve life. For these two years has the famine been in the land: and yet there are five years, in the which there shall neither be earing nor harvest. And ELOHIYM sent me before you to preserve you a posterity in the earth, and to save your lives by a great deliverance.

Genesis 45:4-7

"And Elohiym sent me before you to preserve you a posterity in the earth, and to save your lives by a *great deliverance.*"

Yoseph is a model of the Messiah who was to come to bring deliverance to those who would believe, and so it has been now for two thousand years.

As it was at this time, so shall it be again, that our Messiah should arrange deliverance for us. The prophecy continues:

Thus says your son Yoceph, ELOHIYM has made me lord of all Mitsrayim: come down unto me, tarry not: And you shall dwell in the land of Goshen, and you shall be near unto me, you, and your children, and your children's children, and your flocks, and your herds, and all that you have: And there will I nourish you; for yet there are five years of famine; lest you, and your household, and all that you have, come to poverty.

Genesis 45:9-11

"And you shall dwell in the land of Goshen." The promise is here for deliverance, and for deliverance from the coming five years of famine.

This is the prophecy, and this book is about proclaiming the land of Goshen – a land of deliverance for the remnant, in the heavenlies, that those who call upon the name of Yah'havah might be delivered from that which is coming.

There is more to this prophecy. There is an interesting discussion in Revelation 12:

And I heard a loud voice saying in heaven, Now is come Yeshua, and strength, and the kingdom of our ELOHIYM, and the power of his Mashiach: for the accuser of our brethren is cast down, which accused them before our ELOHIYM day and night. And they overcame him by the blood of the Lamb, and by the word of their testimony; and they loved not their lives unto the death. Therefore rejoice, ye heavens, and ye that dwell in them. Woe to the inhabiters of the earth and of the sea! for the devil is come down unto you, having great wrath, because he knows that he has but a short time. And when the dragon saw that he was cast unto the earth, he persecuted the woman which brought forth the man child. And to the woman were given two wings of a great eagle, that she might fly into the wilderness, into her place, where she is nourished for a time, and times, and half a time, from the face of the serpent. And the serpent cast out of his mouth water as a flood after the woman, that he might cause her to be carried away of the flood. And the earth helped the woman, and the earth opened her mouth, and swallowed up the flood which the dragon cast out of his mouth.

Revelation 12:10-16

The woman which has a crown of twelve stars on her head is taken into a wilderness for a time, times, and half a time. Prophetically, this is 3½ prophetic years, or 42 months, or 1,260 days. This is again a prophecy concerning the twelve tribes of Yisra'el and the departure into a wilderness where they will receive divine protection for a period of 3½ years. Is the wilderness knowable?

When you ask, "where can we go?" the answer is being revealed. Come down to Goshen.

Chapter Two

Who is Yisra'el?

Who is Yisra'el? This is a good question, because it is for the lost sheep of the house of Yisra'el with whom Yeshua was sent.

But he answered and said, I am not sent but unto the lost sheep of the house of Yisra'el.

Matthew 15:24

Here, the Messiah spells it out – he is sent unto the lost sheep of the house of Yisra'el. Not only that, be when he sent out the twelve disciples, he sent them out to the lost sheep of the house of Yisra'el:

And when he had called unto him his twelve disciples, he gave them power against unclean spirits, to cast them out, and to heal all manner of sickness and all manner of disease.

. . . 5 These twelve Yeshua sent forth, and commanded them, saying, Go not into the way of the other people, and into any city of the Shomroniym enter ye not: 6 But go rather to the lost sheep of the house of Yisra'el.

Matthew 10:1; 5-6

Who is this house of Yisra'el? Maybe Paul can tell us in Romans chapter 11. We begin by answering the question whether those who are ethnically of the house of Judah, Benjamin and Levi are included in the house of Yisra'el:

Has ELOHIYM cast away his people? ELOHIYM forbid. For I also am an Yisra`e'liy, of the seed of Avraham, of the tribe of Binyamiyn. ELOHIYM has not cast away his people which he foreknew.

Romans 11:1-2

In Romans 11, Paul tells us of the plight of the house of Yisra'el – a group sent into diaspora well ahead of the house of Judah, intermingled with other people (sometimes called gentiles) which Paul refers to as the wild branch of the olive tree.

For if the firstfruit be holy, the lump is also holy: and if the root be holy, so are the branches. 17 And if some of the branches be broken off, and you, being a wild olive tree, were graffed in among them, and with them partake of the root and fatness of the olive tree; 18 Boast not against the branches. But if you boast, you bear not the root, but the root you. 19 You will say then, The branches were broken off, that I might be graffed in. 20 Well; because of unbelief they were broken off, and you stand by faith. Be not highminded, but fear: **21** For if ELOHIYM spared not the natural branches, take heed lest he also spare not you.

Romans 11:16-21

Here, Paul is telling us that anyone of the other people can be grafted in to the root of the olive tree, be he goes on to tell us that you remain grafted in only so long as you continue in his goodness: "otherwise you shall also be cut off." Romans 11:22.

But Paul tells us that in addition to the intermingled other people of the dispersed house of Yisra'el (the ten northern tribes), the house of Judah will also be redeemed in the whole of the house of Yisra'el.

And they also, if they abide not still in unbelief, shall be graffed in: for ELOHIYM is able to graff them in again. **24** *For if you were cut out of the olive tree which is wild by nature, and were graffed contrary to nature into a good olive tree: how much more shall these, which be the natural branches, be graffed into their own olive tree?* **25** *For I would not, brethren, that ye should be ignorant of this mystery, lest ye should be wise in your own conceits; that blindness in part is happened to Yisra'el, until the fulness of the other people be come in.*

Romans 11:23-25

And so Paul tells us that "all Yisra'el shall be saved: as it is written, There shall come out of Siy'on the Deliverer, and shall turn away unElohiymliness from Ya'aqov (Yisra'el): for this is my covenant unto them, when I shall take away their sins."

Romans 11:26-27

Such powerful words. It is Yeshua who brings deliverance, and it is your confession of Him that brings you into Yisra'el.

Chapter Three

Who is the remnant?

Who is the remnant that Elohiym is preserving in these end times? As it was written above, all those who call upon the name of Yah'havah. Some of you may be asking about this name, so I will take a second to explain.

For many people, there is only one name in their faith, and it is the name of Jesus. While I understand this conviction (for there is no other name under heaven by which men are saved), we should call Him by his birth name, which is Yeshua (some say Yehoshua), which means salvation. Many of you already use this name, because you already know that Yah'havah has already called you into the remnant.

However, Yeshua Himself called us to pray unto the Father – Abba - saying "hallowed be your name." Yeshua clearly knows of the name of the Father, which was given to us as the tetragrammaton יהוה. This name is often pronounced Yahweh, but there is no scriptural or linguistic support for this. Yah is the shortened version, but the longer version Yah'havah does two things: it includes the breath of the father (hah) in the name – the same breath inserted in the name of Abram - and it gives the complete meaning of the name, which is "I Am He who breathes life."

Keep in mind what Yeshua said in Matthew 7:

*Not everyone that says unto me, ADONAI, ADONAI, shall enter into the kingdom of heaven; but he that does the will of my Father which is in heaven. **22** Many will say to me in that day, ADONAI, ADONAI, have we not prophesied in your name? and in your name have cast out devils? and in your name done many wonderful works? **23** And then will I profess unto them, I never knew you: depart from me, ye transgressors of the Torah.*

Matthew 7:21-23

So who is the remnant? Satan knows, for he comes to make war with them in the last days:

*And I heard a loud voice saying in heaven, Now is come Yeshua, and strength, and the kingdom of our ELOHIYM, and the power of his Mashiach: for the accuser of our brethren is cast down, which accused them before our ELOHIYM day and night. **11** And they overcame him by the blood of the Lamb, and by the word of their testimony; and they loved not their lives unto the death. **12** Therefore rejoice, ye heavens, and ye that dwell in* them. *Woe to the inhabiters of the earth and of the sea! for the devil is come down unto you, having great wrath, because he knows that he has but a short time. **13** And when the dragon saw that he was cast unto the earth, he persecuted the woman which brought forth the man child. **14** And to the woman were given two wings of a great eagle, that she might fly into the wilderness, into her place, where she is nourished for a time, and times, and half a time, from the face of the serpent. **15** And the serpent cast out of his mouth water as a flood after the woman, that he might cause her to be carried away of the flood. **16** And the earth helped the woman, and the earth opened her mouth, and swallowed up the flood which the dragon cast out of his mouth. **17** And the dragon was wroth with the woman, and went to make war with **the remnant of her seed, which keep the commandments of ELOHIYM, and have the testimony of Yeshua HaMashiach.***

Revelation 12:10-17

The remnant are those "which keep the commandments of Elohiym, and have the testimony of Yeshua HaMashiach."

Who is the remnant?

The Declaration set forth herein concerns these very things, for those of you who are called out; for you, the remnant.

Chapter Four

The Declaration

When, by divine intervention and by the will of יהוה it becomes necessary for the remnant of the called out assembly to assume among the governing bodies of the earth a separate governance to which the Laws of Nature and the Commandments, Ordinances, Statutes and Judgments of יהוה compel them, and to set forth the tenets of ordered liberty, the undersigned now proclaim the territory of the Columbia River basin and its tributaries to be the land of Goshen, and proclaim citizenship therein on the following terms and conditions:

Article I

All governing authorities at each and every level of government or in any position of authority whatsoever established, created, exercising authority in, or otherwise in existence in Goshen (hereafter, the "Governing Body") shall be subject unto the higher powers. For there is no power but of ELOHIYM: the powers that be are ordained of ELOHIYM. Whosoever violates this provision is without lawful authority to act in governance.

Article II

No law, rule, code, statute, ordinance, command, decree, judgment or edict of any sort is binding, lawful, or authoritative, if it violates these Articles of this Declaration.

Article III

No law, ordinance, command, decree, judgment or edict that denies or contradicts the existence of Yah'havah Elohiym יהוה אֱלֹהִים shall be enacted or established.

Article IV

No law, rule, code, statute, ordinance, command, decree, judgment or edict of any sort shall be created or established as Elohiyms or other objects of worship before Yah'havah Elohiym יהוה אֱלֹהִים.

Article V

No law, rule, code, statute, ordinance, command, decree, judgment or edict of any sort shall be created or established to cause any person to bow down to or to serve any graven images, nor shall the Governing Body cause any likeness of anything that is in heaven above, or that *is* in the earth beneath, or that *is* in the water under the earth to be worshipped.

Article VI

The name of Yah'havah Elohiym יהוה אֱלֹהִים shall not be used for any profane purpose.

Article VII

The Sabbath day shall be established from sundown on Friday to sundown on Saturday, and it shall be kept set apart, providing for six days of labor, and a seventh day of rest for every person.

Article VIII

No law, rule, code, statute, ordinance, command, decree, judgment or edict of any sort shall be created or established to cause dishonor for a father or a mother.

Article IX

Life is sacred from conception to natural death, and no law, rule, code, statute, ordinance, command, decree, judgment or edict of any sort shall be created or established to provide for the taking of human life, except in restoration for the taking of another life.

Article X

No law, rule, code, statute, ordinance, command, decree, judgment or edict of any sort shall be created or established that allows for the breaking of wedlock except for sexual immorality or abandonment.

Article XI

No law, rule, code, statute, ordinance, command, decree, judgment or edict of any sort shall be created or established that provides for the transfer of a person's house, a person's spouse, a person's employees, a person's animal stock, a person's equipment, a person's money, a person's wealth, a person's intellectual property, a person's personal property, a person's real property, or anything else that belongs to a person to another person or group of persons, including a transfer to the Governing Body.

Article XII

No law, rule, code, statute, ordinance, command, decree, judgment or edict of any sort shall be created or established that allows for false witness, including any law allowing libel, defamation, or perjury.

Article XIV

No law, rule, code, statute, ordinance, command, decree, judgment or edict of any sort shall be created or established that causes or encourages a person to covet a person's house, a person's spouse, a person's employees, a person's animal stock, a person's equipment, a person's money, a person's wealth, a person's intellectual property, a person's personal property, a person's real property, or anything else that belongs to a person.

Article XV

No law, rule, code, statute, ordinance, command, decree, judgment or edict of any sort shall be created or established that provides for a fiat currency, that provides for any money other than gold and silver coin, or that imposes an interest rate on money.

Article XVI

The Governing Body is expressly prohibited from owning or controlling real property, and the taxation of property is expressly prohibited.

Article XVII

Progressive taxes, or any tax that imposes a higher percentage on one person over another is expressly prohibited.

Article XVIII

The cumulative tax imposed from any source whatsoever, when combined with all other taxes, user fees, or other fees collected by the Governing Body shall not exceed Thirteen and one-third percent (13.3%) of any amount subject to tax.

Article XIX

The feasts of Yah'havah shall be duly ratified by edict of the Governing Body, the Sabbaths shall be declared, and the feasts of Passover, Unleavened Bread, First fruits, Shevuot (Pentecost), Trumpets, Atonement and Tabernacles shall be declared.

Article XX

The ancient calendar shall be duly ratified and established by the Governing Body, and the Gregorian calendar shall no longer be used. The first month shall begin on the first zero moon following the vernal equinox, and each new month shall begin on the zero moon thereafter.

Article XIX

Citizenship in Goshen shall be predicated upon an open confession of faith in the atoning grace of Yeshua HaMashiach and an affirmation of covenant to uphold His commandments, expressed in the taking of the cup and the eating of the broken bread.

Chapter Five
The Laws of Nature

The laws of nature necessary to the tenets of ordered liberty and the governance of the land of Goshen are the metaphysical truths related to human interaction. Although there are many such truths, the principals necessary within the land of Goshen are a simple roster of ten. These laws of nature constitute the metaphysical underpinning of law upon which we are justified as a civil body, and are to be respected.

We, the citizens of Goshen, therefore declare the following principals, also known as the laws of nature, to be binding in Goshen:

First principal:

Yah'havah Elohiym יהוה אֱלֹהִים

It is this principal that is the first principal upon which all education, science, art, and theology is properly based. The premise is stated in the following syllogism:

Assuming *Elohiym*, we have concluded *Elohiym*.

This premise then allows the disciple to seek to discover that which Elohiym has done. In comparison, modern science sought to discover that which has occurred assuming no Elohiym.

Second principal:

Faithfulness

We are called to be faithful to Yah'havah Elohiym, being certain to hold Him first in priority above all other things. This necessity of this principal is best expressed by the apostle James.

A double minded man is unstable in all his ways.

James 1:8

Or consider another discussion by James of the lack of faithfulness:

For if any be a hearer of the word, and not a doer, he is like unto a man beholding his natural face in a glass: For he beholds himself, and goes his way, and straightway forgets what manner of man he was.

James 1:23-24

We are called to adhere to and remain in a covenant relationship with Elohiym, being faithful without placing idols before him. Politically, the state must be restricted from creating its own idols and requiring the citizens to worship them.

Third principal:

Reverence.

When the first two principals are in place, it is the proper part of civil society to revere His name. Reverence to the name is called for by Yeshua HaMashiach:

Our Father, which art in heaven, hallowed be your name.

Matthew 6:9

Know this, that the name of the Father is

Yah'havah Elohiym יהוה אֱלֹהִים

The name of the Son is Yeshua HaMashiach.

The Holy Spirit is called the Ruach HaQodesh or Ruach Elohiym (the Spirit of Elohiym).

Fourth principal:

Rhythm of life.

We are called to keep one day in seven for rest, called the Sabbath. We are called to keep one year in seven for rest. We are called to celebrate seven feasts, and to do so in accord with a lunar/solar calendar. These are the markers of the rhythm of life.

Fifth principal:

Honor.

We are called to honor and not curse, to honor our heritage in our fathers and mothers, and to honor one another. To honor is to bless in Spirit and Truth.

Sixth principal:

Life.

Life is in the blood, and all life which carries blood is sacred and cannot be taken except by the express command of the Father.

Seventh principal:

Wedlock.

A man is called to leave his mother and father and to cleave unto his woman in a covenant of wedlock, wedlock should not be broken, and this covenant is to be honored in Spirit and in truth.

Eighth principal:

Property.

We are called to honor the property rights of others, including the care, custody, and control of the person's house and land, the person's wedlock relationship, the person's employee contracts, the person's animal stock, the person's equipment, the person's money, the person's wealth, the person's intellectual property, the person's personal property, the person's real property, or anything else that belongs to the person.

Ninth principal

Honesty.

We are called to speak the truth and to bear a true witness and a true testimony; to not bear false witness; to not give perjury; to not defame or libel; and to not establish ill-repute by false means, but to carry the testimony of Yeshua HaMashiach in Spirit and in Truth.

Tenth principal:

Respect.

We are called to not covet but to respect the property rights of others, including the care, custody, and control of the person's house and land, the person's wedlock relationship, the person's employee contracts, the person's animal stock, the person's equipment, the person's money, the person's wealth, the person's intellectual property, the person's personal property, the person's real property, or anything else that belongs to the person.

Chapter Six

The Laws of Nature's Elohiym

Therefore know this day, and consider it in your heart, that the Lord Himself is Elohiym in heaven above and on the earth beneath; there is no other. You shall therefore keep His statutes and His commandments which I command you today, that it may go well with you and with your children after you, and that you may prolong your days in the land which the Lord your Elohiym is giving you for all time.

Deuteronomy 4:39-40

The laws of nature's Elohiym that are necessary to the governance of the land of Goshen are the commands, ordinances, statutes and judgments of Elohiym, as set forth in the Sacred Scriptures. While some may say this is the Torah (the instruction), such a phrase must include the teaching of HaMashiach, and is better expressed as the Torah Fulfilled.

Think not that I am come to destroy the Torah, or the prophets: I am not come to destroy, but to fulfil. **18** *For verily I say unto you, Till heaven and earth pass, one jot or one tittle shall in no wise pass from the Torah, till* *all be fulfilled. Whosoever therefore shall break one of these least commandments, and shall teach men so, he shall be called the least in the kingdom of heaven: but whosoever shall do and teach them, the same shall be called great in the kingdom of heaven. For I say unto you, That except your righteousness shall exceed the righteousness of the scribes and Parashiym, ye shall in no case enter into the kingdom of heaven.*

Matthew 5:17-20

We, the citizens of Goshen, therefore declare the Torah Fulfilled, the Sacred Scriptures of the House of Yisra'el, also known as the laws of Nature's Elohiym, to be binding in Goshen.

And one of the scribes came, and having heard them reasoning together, and perceiving that he had answered them well, asked him, Which is the first commandment of all? And Yeshua answered him, The first of all the commandments is, Hear, O Yisra'el; YAH'HAVAH our ELOHIYM is one YAH'HAVAH: And you shall love YAH'HAVAH your ELOHIYM with all your heart, and with all your soul, and with all your mind, and with all your strength: this is the first commandment. And the second is like, namely this, You shall love your neighbour as yourself. There is none other commandment greater than these. And the scribe said unto him, Well, Master, you have said the truth: for there is one ELOHIYM; and there is none other but he: And to love him with all the heart, and with all the understanding, and with all the soul, and with all the strength, and to love his neighbour as himself, is more than all whole burnt offerings and sacrifices. And when Yeshua saw that he answered discreetly, he said unto him, You are not far from the kingdom of ELOHIYM. And no man after that dared ask him any question.

Mark 12:28-34

Chapter Seven
The Declaration of Rights

We, the citizens of Goshen, recognize, declare, and codify the following rights for each and every human being, from conception to natural death, and declare such rights to be inalienable, and incapable of waiver in Goshen.

Right No. 1

The right to worship the one true Elohiym

Right No. 2

The right to hold Elohiym as superior to all other moral authority.

Right No. 3

The right to be free from worshipping man-made things.

Right No. 4

The right to speak without misusing the name of our Elohiym.

Right No. 5

The right to life.

Right No. 6

The right to be free from being murdered.

Right No. 7

The right to be free from and the right to redress false gossip.

Right No. 8

The right to be free from and the right redress perjury.

Right No. 9

The right to be free from and the right to redress false accusations.

Right No. 10

The right to be free from and the right to redress false defamatory or libelous statements.

Right No. 11

The right to ordered liberty.

Right No. 12

The right to work six out of seven days.

Right No. 13

The right to take one day in seven off from work.

Right No. 14

The right to give our employees one day in seven off from work.

Right No. 15

The right to own, possess and use property.

Right No. 16

The right to be free from the theft of our property.

Right No. 17

The right to be free from the theft of our houses.

Right No. 18

The right to be free from the theft of our marriages.

Right No. 19

The right to be free from the theft of our employees.

Right No. 20

The right to be free from the theft of our means of production.

Right No. 21

The right to be free from the theft of our families.

Right No. 22

The right to be free from the theft of everything else that rightfully belongs to us.

Right No. 23

The right to marriage and family.

Right No. 24

The right to be free from adultery.

Right No. 25

The right to honor our mothers.

Right No. 26

The right to honor our fathers.

Right No. 27

The right to self-defense.

Right No. 28

The right to be free from interference with our houses.

Right No. 29

The right to be free from interference with our spouses.

Right No. 30

The right to be free from interference with our employees.

Right No. 31

The right to be free from interference with our means of production.

Right No. 32

The right to be free from interference with anything that rightfully belongs to us.

Chapter Eight

Citizenship in Goshen

*Behold, the days come, says YAH'HAVAH, that I
will make a Renewed Covenant with the house of Yisra'el,
and with the house of Yahudah:* **32** *Not according to the
covenant that I made with their fathers in the day that I
took them by the hand to bring them out of the land of
Mitsrayim; which my covenant they broke, although I was
a man unto them, says YAH'HAVAH:* **33** *But this shall be
the covenant that I will make with the house of Yisra'el;
After those days, says YAH'HAVAH, I will put my Torah in
their inward parts, and write it in their hearts; and will
be their ELOHIYM, and they shall be my people.* **34** *And
they shall teach no more every man his neighbour, and
every man his brother, saying, Know YAH'HAVAH: for
they shall all know me, from the least of them unto the
greatest of them, says YAH'HAVAH: for I will forgive their
iniquity, and I will remember their sin no more.*

Jeremiah 31:31-34

*Behold, the days come, says YAH'HAVAH, when I
will make a Renewed Covenant with the house of Yisra'el
and with the house of Yahudah:* **9** *Not according to the*

covenant that I made with their fathers in the day when I took them by the hand to lead them out of the land of Mitsrayim; because they continued not in my covenant, and I regarded them not, says YAH'HAVAH. **10** For this is the covenant that I will make with the house of Yisra'el after those days, says YAH'HAVAH; I will put my Torah into their mind, and write it in their hearts: and I will be to them an ELOHIYM, and they shall be to me a people: **11** And they shall not teach every man his neighbour, and every man his brother, saying, Know YAH'HAVAH: for all shall know me, from the least to the greatest. **12** For I will be merciful to their unrighteousness, and their sins and their lawlessness will I remember no more.

Hebrews 8:8-12

Brethren, my heart's desire and prayer to ELOHIYM for Yisra'el is, that they might be saved. **2** For I bear them record that they have a zeal of ELOHIYM, but not according to knowledge. **3** For they being ignorant of ELOHIYM'S righteousness, and going about to establish their own righteousness, have not submitted themselves unto the righteousness of ELOHIYM. **4** For HaMashiach is the fulfillment of the Torah for righteousness to everyone that believes. **5** For Mosheh describes the righteousness which is of the Torah, That the man which does those *things shall live by them.* **6** *But the righteousness which is of faith speaks on this wise, Say not in your heart, Who shall ascend into heaven? (that is, to bring HaMashiach down from above:)* **7** *Or, Who shall descend into the deep? (that is, to bring up HaMashiach again from the dead.)* **8** *But what says it? The word is nigh you, even in your mouth, and in your heart: that is, the word of faith, which we preach;* **9** *That if you shall confess with your mouth ADONAI Yeshua, and shall believe in your heart that ELOHIYM has raised him from the dead, you shall be saved.* **10** *For with the heart man believes unto righteousness; and with the mouth confession is made unto Yeshua.* **11** *For the scripture says, Whosoever believes on him shall not be ashamed.* **12** *For there is no difference between the Yahudiy and the Greek: for the same ADONAI over all is rich unto all that call upon him.* **13** *For whosoever shall call upon the name of YAH'HAVAH shall be saved.*

Romans 10:1-13

Goshen is a spiritual place, and a physical place, a place in the wilderness reserved by Yah'havah for his people where they shall be delivered. Therefore, deliverance to Goshen begins with the call upon the name Yah'havah Elohiym Tsavuot.

Paul also tells us that you must confess Adonai Yeshua with your mouth and believe in your heart that Elohiym raised Him from the dead.

The gift of the Holy Spirit is that the Torah has been written into your mind and poured into your heart. If these things are true about you, then you are a citizen of Goshen.

Say unto your brethren, This do ye; lade your beasts, and go, get you unto the land of Kena`an; **18** *And take your father and your households, and come unto me: and I will give you the good of the land of Mitsrayim, and ye shall eat the fat of the land.* **19** *Now you are commanded, this do ye; take you wagons out of the land of Mitsrayim for your little ones, and for your women, and bring your father, and come.* **20** *Also regard not your stuff; for the good of all the land of Mitsrayim is yours.* **21** *And the children of Yisra'el did so: and Yoceph gave them wagons, according to the commandment of Pharaoh, and gave them provision for the way.*

Genesis 45:17-21

Come down unto me and tarry not; And you shall dwell in the land of Goshen, and you shall be near unto me, you, and your children, and your children's children, and your flocks, and your herds, and all that you have:

And there will I nourish you; for yet there are five years of famine; lest you, and your household, and all that you have, come to poverty.

Genesis 45:9-11